CONTENTS

Front cover: *Scatophagus argus.* Photo by H.J. Richter.

Front endpaper: *Brachygobius nunus.* Photo by Hans Joachim Richter.

Frontis: *Poecilia petenensis.* Photo courtesy of the New York Zoological Society.

Back endpaper: *Scatophagus argus.* Photo by R. Zukal.

Back cover: *Monodactylus argenteus* and *Scatophagus argus.*

ISBN 0-87666-519-9

Distributed in the U.S. by T.F.H. Publications, Inc., 211 West Sylvania Avenue, PO Box 427, Neptune, NJ 07753; in England by T.F.H. (Gt. Britain) Ltd., 13 Nutley Lane, Reigate, Surrey; in Canada to the book store and library trade by Beaverbooks Ltd., 150 Lesmill Road, Don Mills, Ontario M38 2T5, Canada; in Canada to the pet trade by Rolf C. Hagen Ltd., 3225 Sartelon Street, Montreal 382, Quebec; in Southeast Asia by Y.W. Ong, 9 Loring 36 Geylang, Singapore 14; in Australia and the South Pacific by Pet Imports Pty. Ltd., P.O. Box 149, Brookvale 2100, N.S.W. Australia. Published by T.F.H. Publications, Inc., Ltd., The British Crown Colony of Hong Kong.

BRACKISH
AQUARIUMS

MICHAEL W. GOS

Because of its odd swimming behavior, the tiny bumblebee goby, *Brachygobius nunus,* is one of the most interesting fishes for the brackish water aquarium. Rather than swimming, it literally hops about the aquarium. *Etroplus* species such as the *E. maculatus* shown below guarding its eggs (photo by H.J. Richter) are the only cichlids that are native to Asia, and they live in brackish water.

Introduction

For many years aquarium hobbyists have neglected one of the most interesting and beautiful aspects of the hobby—the brackish water aquarium. Upon setting up our first brackish water tank, we realized that one of the reasons for this neglect is the lack of information on just what brackish water is and what fishes inhabit it. It is amazing to find out how many people believe that brackish means "dirty." It is understandable that they would not want a brackish aquarium in their living room while under this misconception.

1   2

8

Brackish water aquaria are one of the logical specializations into which a hobbyist can advance. This aspect of the hobby takes in the best of both freshwater and marine systems. Many brackish water fishes are as colorful as some marine fishes are, yet they maintain the good points of freshwater fishes: breedability, lower cost, ability to be kept together with live plants and longer life expectancies in the aquarium. Until the aquarist has seen a school of monos in action or watched a figure-eight puffer eat itself into oblivion, he has not yet seen the best the hobby has to offer.

After successfully maintaining a brackish water tank we decided that we could best serve our fellow hobbyists by publishing our techniques. It is the author's hope that this book will help prevent the brackish water novice from having to unnecessarily repeat the research and experimentation that led us to the writing of this book. If it does that, then the reader will save considerable time, effort and money, and this book will have achieved its purpose.

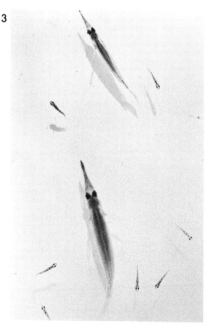

3

(1) There are several species of halfbeaks of the family Hemirhamphidae that are found in brackish water. These are *Dermogenys pusillus*. Photo by M. Chvojka. (2) Some hemirhamphids are live-bearers. Here a female *Dermogenys pusillus* is seen giving birth. The newborn young are quite large compared to those of other aquarium livebearers. (3) A top view of adult halfbeaks and their newborn fry. Photos 2 and 3 by G. Wolfsheimer.

While mollies are most often kept in freshwater in the aquarium, in nature they are more often than not found in brackish waters. Photo by J.P. Kui. While they do much better in brackish water than they do in freshwater, glassfish, such as the *Chanda ranga* seen below, according to the author do not eat well in any aquarium. Photo by H.J. Richter.

What is Brackish Water?

Brackish water can be defined as water that has a salt concentration less than that of seawater. While freshwater has some salt content, it should be understood that the salts we are referring to in this definition are sea salts, predominantly sodium chloride.

If we were to set up a ten-gallon aquarium outdoors and put two gallons of seawater into it, we would soon see one way that brackish water is produced in nature. When it rains, our tank would fill up so that it would eventually contain ten gallons of water, but we should still have only enough salt for two gallons of seawater. The resulting dilution would have a specific gravity of about 1.005, a good density for a brackish water aquarium.

A similar but more common type of dilution occurs in estuaries. Estuaries are formed when seawater is diluted with freshwater near the mouths of rivers or by freshwater springs. Many freshwater and marine fishes occur in these estuaries at some point during their life cycle, and of course, there are some fishes that spend their entire life in this brackish water.

A totally different process often produces brackish rivers and streams. An example of this process was seen in the pre-Aswan-dam Nile River. Prior to the construction of the dam the Nile flooded seasonally depositing organic nutrients on the farmlands and washing away the salts that formed on the soil. The salts then entered the Nile, turning it brackish.

Brackish water can also be formed by non-natural means. In many localities rock salt is spread on the sidewalks in the winter to prevent icing. When the thaws come, the salt travels with runoff water to local streams and rivers, often killing normally freshwater fish.

Many of the fishes that are adapted to brackish water live in neither brackish rivers nor estuaries. These are fish that, because of their physiological makeup, can live in either freshwater, seawater or anything in between. A large part of the commonly kept brackish water fishes fit into this category. They spend part of their time in freshwater rivers, lakes and streams, often entering the open ocean for another part of their lives. Their versatility is evidenced by the way they thrive in both fresh and marine aquaria.

---

(1) A tangle of mangrove roots. Such habitats are found along the coasts in warm climates in estuarine areas. Here the mixing of saltwater and freshwater forms perfect brackish water habitats for many different kinds of fishes. (2) A predatory species found in Asian mangrove habitats is *Datnioides quadrifasciatus.* Because the fish grows to over a foot in length, only young specimens are suitable for aquaria. Photo by Dr. Herbert R. Axelrod.

1
2
3

The definition of brackish water leaves a great deal of leeway with regard to salinity. As most aquarists know, even one teaspoon of salt per gallon is helpful to mollies and monos. However, our research has shown that greater concentrations help even more. The question, then, is: what is the ideal salinity?

Through experimentation, we have obtained our best results using one gallon of seawater to four gallons of freshwater. This produces a hydrometer reading of 1.005. In our research, we have also found that most brackish fishes seem to benefit from fluctuations in salinity, as long as they are

4

(1) Almost the entire skeleton of the glassfish is visible through its transparent flesh. (2) Here a pair of glassfish is engaged in prenuptial behavior. (3) The mummichog, *Fundulus heteroclitus,* is found in brackish waters along the east coast of the U.S.A. It is a good aquarium species. Photos 1, 2 and 3 by Dr. Herbert R. Axelrod. (4) *Aphaniops dispar* is a brackish water killifish found along the coasts of the Middle East. Photo by Dr. G.R. Allen.

not drastic. Since most of them travel between fresh and salt water anyway, this is a normal occurrence for them. Those that stay in brackish water all their lives experience fluctuations due to rainy and dry seasons. The best way for the aquarist to simulate this fluctuation is to replace siphoned water with freshwater only for a time, and then switch to saltwater only for a time. A good range would be 1.002 to 1.007, but the numbers are to serve only as a guideline; you may find a range that works better for you. A final word about salt. Some aquarists spend a substantial amount of money on the tank setup and then try to skimp on the salt. This is a mistake that should be avoided. While any non-iodized table salt works wonders for brackish water fishes, the best results are undoubtedly achieved with a sea salt mix formulated for aquarium use. Common table salt is composed of sodium chloride and dextrose. As can be seen from the table below, sea salts have more ions than just sodium and chlorine. In all, sea water contains about seventy-two elements in varying amounts with fourteen in concentrations larger than 1 ppm.* Of course, many of these elements are very important to the well-being of brackish water fishes. For this reason, we suggest using only salt preparations that contain trace minerals. If a brand that has the trace elements in a separate liquid form is used, we recommend the use of one to two drops of trace elements per gallon of water. In their metabolic processes fishes use up trace elements in the water, and more should be added. This is usually accomplished by making partial water changes but can be done by re-administering a one to two drop dose of liquid trace elements.

MAIN COMPONENTS OF SEAWATER

Positive Ions		Negative Ions	
Sodium	Na$^+$	Chloride	Cl$^-$

---

*ppm = *parts* of a substance (in this case salts) *per million* parts of the solvent (in this case water).

Potassium	K^+	Bicarbonate	HCO_3^-
Magnesium	Mg^{++}	Sulphate	SO_4^{--}
Calcium	Ca^{++}		

Plus about 65 other elements in lesser quantities.

(1) Artificial saltwater mixes are not only good for full marine aquariums, but they also provide a good balance of salts for brackish water fishes. (2) The pH of the brackish water aquarium tends to be a little higher than that which can be measured with most freshwater pH test kits. Saltwater pH test kits such as this are much more useful for monitoring the pH of a brackish water aquarium. (3) Trace elements in marine and brackish water tend to be absorbed by plants and invertebrates. They should be replaced periodically with commercially available trace element solutions.

1

2

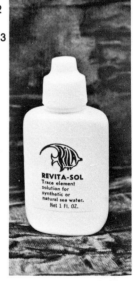

3

The pufferfish *Tetraodon palembangensis* is found in brackish water swamps of Southeast Asia. Archerfishes such as the *Toxotes chatareus* shown below are capable of shooting down insects above the surface with a drop of water.

Getting Started

One of the beauties of the brackish water system is that it can fit into everyone's plans regardless of financial or space limitations. We have kept brackish water tanks as small as five gallons and as large as 100 gallons. The first decision then, is tank size. Since there are several brackish water fishes under two inches long and several over six inches, this choice will later affect the choice of fish.

We strongly recommend the all glass tank with a glass or plastic cover. Salt causes metal, even stainless steel, to rust very rapidly. While the fishes are usually hardy enough to withstand rust pollution, it makes for an unsightly aquarium.

The best filtration system for the brackish water tank is a subsand filter run at full capacity. We personally prefer the full plate type but the tube types work just as well. Running the filter at full capacity serves a dual purpose. It does a better job of filtering the tank, and it adds turbulence to the water. Turbulence is important for several reasons. The water motion simulates the currents of the streams, estuaries and oceans from which the fishes come, surface turbulence increases the amount of dissolved oxygen in the water and it helps to dissipate accumulated carbon dioxide into the atmosphere.

A high amount of dissolved oxygen is required in the brackish water because most brackish water fishes tend to be quite active and because the water temperature is usually kept fairly high. At temperatures slightly above freezing, water has a very high affinity for oxygen, but as the temperature rises this affinity begins to drop. Freshwater and marine aquaria are normally kept in the low to mid seventies, but brackish water tanks should be kept at about 80°F. This higher temperature means less oxygen for more active fishes.

Good surface turbulence also accomplishes another task. Fishes having a high metabolic rate release excessive amounts of carbon dioxide into the water. This gas leaves the water in two ways: by surface turbulence and absorption by photosynthesizing plants. Since many brackish water fishes are plant eaters, thereby creating problems with keeping plants, the turbulence takes on added importance.

As mentioned before, most brackish water fishes are very hardy. As a result they can stand much greater variations in pH and hardness than can most freshwater or saltwater fishes. Nevertheless, our original purpose in setting up a brackish water tank was to simulate as closely as possible the actual conditions the fishes encounter in the wild.

In nature, both pH and water hardness vary, but generally brackish water (with low salt content) is fairly hard and has a pH of around 7.6; seawater is also relatively hard but has a pH of about 8.3. As we increase salt content we should try to increase pH. If the aquarist uses commercial sea salt, and the hardness takes care of itself, since the salt contains pH buffers as well as water hardening minerals such as carbonates and sulphates. As more salt is added, more buffers are added and the pH and hardness rise accordingly.

With either freshwater or saltwater fishes, the aquarist sets up his tank with freshwater or saltwater and then puts in the fishes. With brackish water tanks, it's a little more complicated. Very few local dealers keep brackish water fishes in brackish water. Since these fishes generally sell out rapidly, most dealers adapt them to freshwater and advise their customers to add some salt to their water. For a few days 100% freshwater will not harm most brackish water fishes very much. Other dealers keep some or all brackish water fishes in salt water. The hobbyist, therefore, must determine the properties of the water in his dealer's tanks and set up his own as close to those properties as possible. After the fishes have been placed in the tank and have had a day or two to acclimate to the water, the water can then be adjusted toward the brackish side. Starting with freshwater, add a few tablespoons or more of salt daily until the desired specific gravity is reached. The daily amounts should be small in a small tank and more substantial in a larger tank. If the original water was marine, the hobbyist should siphon a little out each day and replace it with freshwater until the desired salinity is reached. Once the desired salinity is reached, the specific gravity should be allowed to stay where it is for a week or so, and then the salinity fluctuations we recommended earlier can be started.

One of the best plants for the brackish water aquarium is *Hygrophila polysperma.* Photo by T.J. Horeman. The scats and monodactyls shown below are being kept without plants other than algae, since they are avid plant eaters. Photo by Dr. D. Terver, Nancy Aquarium, France.

Plants for the Brackish Water Aquarium

Maintaining plants in the brackish aquarium is easily accomplished, but a few differences from the methods used in freshwater tanks must be kept in mind for the aquarist to successfully propagate them.

Salt affects plants in much the same way it does fishes. We know that both plants and animals maintain a certain concentration of salt in each and every cell. This salt is dissolved in fluids within the cell. A living plant can either isolate itself from its environment by impervious cell walls,

or attempt to maintain a salinity similar to that of the outside environment. But a problem occurs because of the size of the pores in the cell wall. They are large enough for water molecules to move in and out freely, but the salt molecules are often there to stay. As a result, any changes must be accomplished by pumping water in or out of the cell. Most of the common freshwater plants are designed to live in freshwater, and if slight amounts of salt are added to the water, the cells must adjust. Since the salt concentration on the outside cannot be brought in through the cell wall, the cells give up some of their water in attempt to dilute the salt concentration outside the cell. This of course causes dehydration of the cells. Many of our hardier plants can stand a small degree of dehydration, but obviously the plant cells cannot make an appreciable change in the outside concentration. They simply do not contain enough water. If the plant is hardy and can stand the difference, it survives.

There are very few common aquarium plants that are ideal for a brackish aquarium, but in general, waxy-leaved plants have the best chance of survival, since the coating on the leaves insulates them against the environment. Therefore, plants like giant sagittaria, *Sagittaria gigantea,* are a good choice. Java fern, *Microsorium pteropus,* while sometimes hard to locate, also does quite well in a brackish aquarium.

Salinity is only one of the problems faced by plants in the brackish water aquarium. As mentioned earlier, the high metabolic rate and the high activity level of brackish water fishes accompanied by high water temperatures creates the need for heavy filtration; this naturally creates high turbulence. The filtration and the turbulence can wreak havoc with the plants. In the case of undergravel filters (which are the best kind to use where the fishes' welfare is concerned) they may be too efficient for the plants' own good. In the removal and break down of waste matter, they do such a thorough job that not enough nutrients are left over for fertilizer. The plants, therefore, may live in a state of hunger. This problem can be overcome by planting them in pots. In this way the gravel around the roots is not subject to such heavy filtration and the waste matter can decompose slowly.

Solving the turbulence problem is considerably more difficult. The best way seems to be to stick with tougher plants that can withstand the moving water. Using an airstone in the undergravel filter can move more water with less air, resulting in smaller bubbles and a reduction of turbulence. The problem with this method is that the filters with airstones are nearly twice the price of the ones with smaller tubes.

Several of the brackish water fishes are active plant eaters and can devastate an entire tank full of plants in a matter of days. Particular problems occur if schools of mollies or scats are maintained. Mollies can strip the leaves off many of the smaller plants, although they usually will do no noticeable damage to giant sag or other large plants. Scats, on the other hand, when placed several to a tank, devastate plants. The best remedy is to use plastic plants or a rocky decor with no plants. Such decor can be very attractive if done properly.

One last problem encountered by aquarists is the uprooting of plants due to active fishes and gravel diggers. As is the case with some of the larger cichids, the plants may be anchored under a rock or attached to a tube type undergravel filter with monofilament fishing line.

The plants discussed in this chapter are those with which we have had the most success in our brackish water tanks, and they are those which the average beginner may keep with a reasonable chance for success. It is by no means a complete list, and someone who is especially good with aquatic plants can probably do well with more.

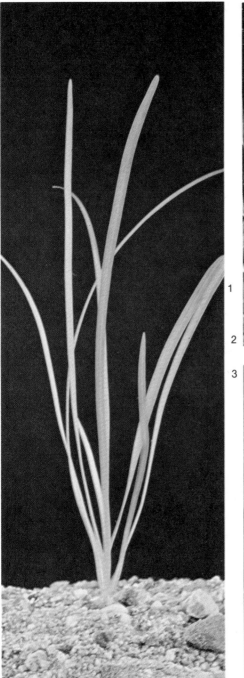

4

5

Some good plants for the brackish water aquarium are: (1) *Sagittaria subulata;* (2) *Vallisneria americana;* (3) *Vallisneria gigantea* (flower shown); (4) pigmy chain swordplant, *Echinodorus tenellus;* (5) *Sagittaria graminea.* Photo 2 by T.J. Horeman; all other photos by R. Zukal.

PIGMY CHAIN SWORDPLANT
(ECHINODORUS TENELLUS)

Although this three- to four-inch plant is said to need soft acid water, it has been our experience that it will do fine in a brackish tank with small fishes that will not uproot it. The pigmy chain swordplant reproduces rapidly by means of runners. Under good conditions it can completely carpet a tank bottom in a matter of months. In a very small tank housing halfbeaks, glassfishes, gobies or the like, the runners can be removed and one plant coaxed into filling out and becoming a short center plant.

The pigmy chain swordplant, from the tropical areas of the western hemisphere, needs bright light but not direct sunlight. For best results, the bottom gravel should have some peat mixed in. Care must be taken in planting so that the crown of the plant is not covered by the substrate. A good way to accomplish this is to bury the plant deeper than it should be and then gently pull it up until the crown is just above the gravel.

WATER SPRITE
(CERATOPTERIS THALICROIDES)

This plant can take on three entirely different forms depending upon environmental conditions. If it is just dropped into the tank, it develops round leaves and remains afloat at the surface. If it is left floating long enough, the roots will grow down into the gravel. On the other hand, if it is planted in the gravel it comes to resemble a carrot plant. In this form it can take one of two shapes, one with a thin frilly leaf, or the second with a bulkier, deeply cut leaf. As the plant matures, the tall leaves develop new plants at the water surface. New leaves unroll in fernlike fashion and can develop completely in two days. The only real drawback with this plant is that in its reproductive zeal it gives the tank a messy appearance. Being soft, it is also a prime target for plant-eating fishes and snails. Water sprite is found in tropical areas worldwide. As a result, it should have water temperatures of 77°F. or more. Under ideal conditions with bright light, the plant can grow to 18 inches in height.

VALLISNERIA SPECIES

Vallisneria is one of the two aquarium grasses available. It can be easily distinguished from the *Sagittaria* species by the presence of a light green stripe running down the center of each leaf. The American variety is very large and not often available. Most of the species commonly kept are European. It is said that *Vallisneria* does not do well in the presence of other plants, especially *Sagittaria*. It is our experience, however, that they thrive alongside most common aquarium plants provided they are not in competition for light. The giant variety *(V. gigantea)* can grow up to six feet in length, and as such is not suitable for home aquaria. The common Italian val *V. spiralis* reaches 18 inches in length, and the "torta" species *(V. americana)* 12 inches. The common varieties need a very strong light, but the "torta" will do best in a subdued light and warmer temperatures. Like the pigmy chain swordplant, the soft leaves are favorites of the plant eaters.

HYGROPHILA SPECIES

Hygrophila polysperma is one of the three ideal plants for the brackish aquarium. It seems to be able to withstand almost anything and is usually left alone by the plant eaters. It should be planted as a bunch plant and, as with all bunch plants, the bottom inch or so should be removed along with the leaves on the bottom two inches before planting. The plant appears to die almost immediately but catches on in a few weeks. As it reaches the desired height the tops can be trimmed and planted in order to propagate new plants. This plant originates in India and Malaya and needs bright light to thrive. More light produces larger leaves.

(1) The Java fern, *Microsorium pteropus,* is one of the hardiest brackish water plants. Photo by Dr. D. Terver, Nancy Aquarium, France. (2) The leaves of *Vallisneria gigantea* curl and twist over the surface. (3) Fine-leaved plants such as this *Cabomba* are too delicate for most brackish water aquaria. Photos 2 and 3 by R. Zukal. (4) The spiral threads of *Vallisneria gigantea* carry the flowers. Photo by T.J. Horeman.

4

Probably the most beautiful of all aquarium plants is its cousin, *Hygrophila corymbosa,* or the temple plant, which is characterized by large oval leaves on a central woody stem. It can be propagated in the same manner as *H. polysperma* but grows much faster. The adult plant is 18 to 24 inches high and eight to 10 inches in diameter. Its only drawback is that it, too, is considered a delicacy by the plant eaters.

CABOMBA SPECIES

Cabomba aquatica, although beautiful, is only suitable for tanks with smaller fishes, as the larger ones would demolish it just by swimming past. It requires a strong light source and warm temperatures. It can be propagated by cuttings in much the same way as *Hygrophila* but, due to it's delicacy, is best not transplanted. When the plant grows beyond the desired height, the tops can be cut off and planted. The old plant will then grow a new top. Most of the available species of *Cabomba* are from tropical South America, but there is a North American species sometimes available under the name *Cabomba caroliniana.* It has a much coarser leaf and is not as attractive as *C. aquatica.*

EGERIA DENSA (also called *ANACHARIS* or *ELODEA DENSA*)

Egeria densa is probably the best beginning plant, as it is nearly indestructible if given at least eight hours of strong light daily. Its best feature for brackish use is its ability to take nutrients directly from the water rather than having to draw them from the gravel. As mentioned earlier, the heavy filtration necessary in the brackish water tank can starve most plants, but *Egeria* is not affected. If there is a weak point to this plant, it is its attractiveness to hungry scats. But since it can grow up to an inch a day, even this point is not much of a detriment.

HORNWORT *(CERATOPHYLLUM DEMERSUM)*

This would be the perfect aquarium plant if it had roots. Not only is it one of the most beautiful of background plants, but also it is the perfect spawning medium for almost every plant-spawning fish in the hobby today. For tops in appearance, anchor the center of the plant and allow both ends to cascade to the surface. If possible, anchor it under a rock so the larger fishes will not uproot it.

Hornwort is very common and grows in all tropical and temperate areas of the world. The author has collected strands in excess of ten feet in length from cold Missouri lakes.

While a very strong light is required to keep the color dark and the plant growing, direct sunlight should be avoided since it will cause algal growth that can kill the plant.

SAGITTARIA SPECIES

All the *Sagittaria* species are similar in requirements to *Vallisneria* species, but they are better suited to brackish aquarium use. They need clean water and lots of light, both of which are easy to achieve. They seem to be almost immune to salt, as their waxy coating provides plenty of protection.

The hardiest of grasses, *Sagittaria* does best in a substrate of sand and clay mix. In the largest tanks, the giant variety is truly impressive. Regardless of which variety is chosen, the leaves are stiff and stand up better to the assaults of plant eaters.

For a hardier carpet than pigmy chain swordplants, dwarf *Sagittaria* species such as *S. subulata* provide the perfect alternative. Chances of success with plants are greatly improved if the brackish water tank is filled with *Sagittaria*.

2

3

34

(1) Pigmy chain swordplant and runners. (2) *Egeria densa*. (3) Hornwort, a good spawning medium. (4) *Hygrophila*, a sturdy, decorative plant. (5) *Elodea minor*. (6) *Cabomba* decorative but not good for use in the brackish water aquarium. Photos 2 and 3 by R. Zukal. Photos 1, 4, 5 and 6 by Dr. D. Sculthorpe.

1

2

(1) *Sagittaria* species require strong light. Photo by L.E. Perkins. (2) The deeply incised rooted form of water sprite. (3) Java fern is a true brackish water plant. Photos 2 and 3 by Dr. D. Sculthorpe.

JAVA FERN *(MICROSORIUM PTEROPUS)*

This is by far the best choice for your aquarium as it is the only true brackish water plant available commercially. Even though it can be found in some shops, it is still very rare. The aquarist who locates a starter stock should count himself lucky and spend some time propagating the species for sale.

3

1

2

3

(1) Small scats can be adapted to planted fresh-water aquaria. Photo by Dr. C.W. Emmens. (2) Fine-leaved plants will not survive in a brackish water aquarium. Photo by R. Zukal. (3) Here is a nice assortment of sturdy plants for the brackish aquarium. Photo by the Inman Co. (4) Mono-dactyls can live in marine tanks but do best in brackish water. Photo by Al Schultz. (5) Monos are best kept in groups of at least four. Photo by Dr. Herbert R. Axelrod at Nancy Aquarium, France.

4   5

Rainbowfishes such as *Melanotaenia maccullochi* readily adapt to brackish water. Photo by G. Senfft. Marbled sailfin mollies, such as the one shown below, or any other kinds of mollies thrive and flourish in brackish water. Photo by R. Zukal.

Buying and Acclimating Fishes

Once the tank is set up and the decisions on plants have been made, it is time to add the fishes. The following chapter will give information necessary for the intelligent aquarist to choose the occupants of his tank wisely. Once they are selected and brought home, the most critical part of the process begins.

Acclimation of brackish water fishes always seems to be more difficult than that of either freshwater or saltwater fishes and yet, if the aquarist just makes a few observations and responds accordingly, success can be assured.

(1) A hydrometer is a necessary piece of equipment if one wishes to maintain any consistency in the salinity of a brackish water aquarium. (2) Power filters designed for continuous use will aid in maintaining a healthy aquarium. (3) Digital thermometers are the latest innovation in temperature measuring equipment. They are inexpensive, accurate and durable.

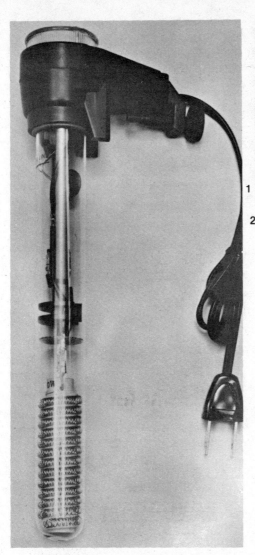

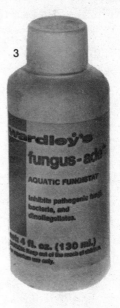

(1) A heater with a good rubber seal like this one has is especially necessary with a brackish or marine aquarium. The disc between the heater element and the thermostat unit gives good temperature control. (2) If fine-leaved vegetation is desired for decorative effects in the brackish water aquarium, plastic plants should be used. (3) *Several basic medicines should be kept at hand but should not be* used indiscriminately.

Fishes are remarkably durable animals. It is truly amazing what they can endure. On many occasions we have sent and received fishes from all over the country by mail with no losses whatsoever. Considering the quality of our rural mail service, this is a truly amazing feat.

A basic knowledge of the handling of fishes goes a long way in ensuring success. Watch the dealer as he nets and bags the fishes. If you are putting out your money for fish, you check it thoroughly in the tank to make sure it is healthy, don't you? Why not make sure it is handled properly, too. The healthiest of fishes can be subject to disease or killed if mishandled.

The net used should be soft and thoroughly wet. If the fish has long flowing fins such as the very fancy mollies or the rare glassfish *Gymnochanda filamentosa,* then it is best moved in a jar instead of a net. That suggestion also goes for any mollie that is pregnant, as the strain of breaking the water surface when moved in a net can cause premature birth.

Once the fish is captured, it is either put directly into a bag of water from its tank or into a jar of the tank water to be later dumped gently into a bag. At this point, the wise aquarist tells the shop owner how he wants his fish packed. If the shop is nearby, the bag can be filled three-quarters full of water with the remainder being filled with air. If the fish is found in a shop several hours from home, there is no reason to pass it by. Filling the bag with just enough water to cover the fish will ensure safe transport for several hours. With the biggest part of the bag filled with air (or oxygen for very long trips), the fish can ride as comfortably as a person in an all day car ride.

To prepare a fish for mail shipment or for a several day ride (in case that rare specimen is found while on vacation), enough water should be put in the largest bag possible to just cover the fish. The rest of the bag should be filled with pure oxygen if possible, but air will often do. It will take up

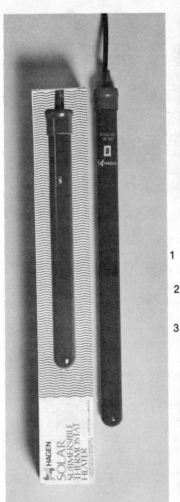

1

2

3

(1) Fully submersible heaters are available for aquarium use. (2) An undergravel filter works well in an uncrowded aquarium. (3) Special power filters are available for intermittent use on small aquaria and continuous use on large aquaria.

(1) Three-spined sticklebacks can be found in coastal waters and adapt well to brackish aquaria. Photo by G. Marcuse. (2) Sticklebacks are nest-building species. Photo by G. Senfft. (3) Strong aeration with medium-sized bubbles provides the brackish aquarium with adequate oxygen. Photo by M.F. Roberts.

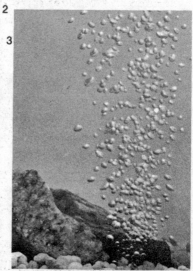

more space, but if the bag is put in a styrofoam bait box the fish will travel well for days. Of course, the more fishes placed in the bag, the faster the oxygen will be depleted and the shorter the time you will have to get them home safely.

Once the fish is brought home it should be acclimated in the way the hobbyist normally acclimates fish. We use the floating bag method and have never had a problem with any of the fishes acclimated in this manner. At this point the aquarist should not become concerned if the fish looks bad. Monos have a way of convincing the beginning aquarist that they are only seconds from death. They turn solid black and immediately hide when introduced to the tank. The next morning they are back to their normal color and are eating every scrap of food in sight. We have found the best way to deal with the anxiety of viewing a poor looking fish is to turn out the light and forget about the tank until morning.

Once the fishes are acclimated to the water, the next step is to get them eating. This is not a problem regularly encountered by the aquarist but can be very frustrating when it does present itself. We have never seen a fish that couldn't be brought around in time. For smaller fishes live brine shrimp generally does the trick. For larger fishes, the best an aquarist can do is to find out what the fishes' food is in the wild and try to duplicate it as closely as possible in the aquarium, and then gradually wean the fishes to more common foods. It is more likely that rather than not eating, the fishes will eat anything in sight (they may even ingest some aquarium gravel). Most of the brackish water fishes have voracious appetites.

Once the fishes are eating, the only other problem that can be anticipated by the aquarist is fighting among the tank residents. If this occurs, it is almost always the fault of the aquarist who made a bad choice of fishes in the first place. Two or three *Monodactylus argenteus* in a tank will invariably fight, but four or more usually school peacefully.

1

2

(1, 2 and 4) Desert water
habitats in the U.S.A.
often have a high ac-
cumulation of salts and
yield interesting fishes.
However, the legality of
the collection of these
fishes should be checked
with the proper wildlife
authorities. (3) The salt-
creek pupfish, *Cyprino-
don salinus,* thrives well
in salty water. Many of
the pupfishes, however,
cannot be taken legally.
Photos by Dr. Martin R.
Brittan.

The larger the school, the more peaceful the fish. Once the fish's ecological needs and behavior are known, the chances of success are greatly increased. The aquarist that puts *Datnioides* and glassfishes in the same tank, for instance, can expect trouble. *Datnioides* are highly predatory and will eat the glassfishes. We cannot overemphasize the importance of knowing your species' requirements prior to purchase.

3 4

Gambusia affinis, a small livebearer, thrives well in brackish swamps. Photo by G. Timmerman. The Australian purple-striped gudgeon, *Mogurnda mogurnda mogurnda,* is one of the brackish water sleeper gobies. Photo by G. Marcuse.

Fishes for the Brackish Water Aquarium

As mentioned earlier, brackish water fishes can either live in brackish water throughout their lives or they can move regularly from fresh to salt with all concentrations in between. Most of the fishes commonly kept in the brackish aquarium hobby are members of the order Perciformes, but other groups are often represented as well. They are very hardy with respect to varying salt concentrations, and the method of varying these concentrations described earlier produces healthy, happy fishes.

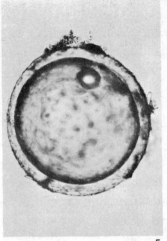 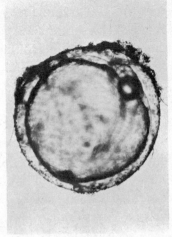

5   6

7

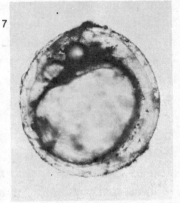

The American flagfish, *Jordanella floridae,* is a colorful killifish commonly found in freshwater and brackish water swamps and channels in Florida and the surrounding area. Photos 1, 2, 3 and 4 are a spawning sequence. The male (front fish) forces the female against thickets of vegetation where eggs are usually expelled and fertilized a few at a time. Photos 5, 6, 7 and 8 show embryonic development of the fish in its transparent egg. In photo 8 the embryo is about 10 days old and the egg is about due to hatch. Photos by K. Nilsson.

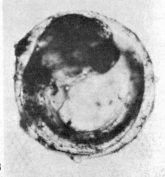

8

Fishes adaptable to brackish water aquariums vary in size from the 1½" bumblebee goby all the way to the 10" *Datnioides* species. Not all are compatible with each other and the aquarist should familiarize himself with the following characteristics before purchasing a fish with which he is unfamiliar.

GLASSFISHES

There are many species of glassfishes. They are generally found near tropical coasts of the Indian and Pacific Oceans. Only the smaller species are kept in the hobby on any sort of a regular basis, and the most common species available are sold as the Indian glassfish. That is the common name given both *Chanda lala* and *Chanda ranga*. Both species are ideal for the small aquarium. They do not do well in an aquarium containing larger fishes and usually starve when in competition for food with them. *Chanda ranga* has a more amber colored body than *C. lala*. In each case the male is easily identified because he is more yellow than the female and his fins are edged in blue.

These fishes get their name from the transparency of their bodies. The organs are contained in a silvery sac in the front half of their body. The back part of the body is clear except for the vertebral column.

Occasionally a hobbyist may run across a rare beauty, *Gymnochanda filamentosa*, with its greatly elongated dorsal and anal fin filaments. Like all glassfishes, *G. filamentosa* has two dorsal fins, but in this case the filaments make it look like there is only one long dorsal fin. This fish is a rare find and should be purchased when it appears in a shop.

Glassfishes spawn upside down just below the surface of the water. The female expels the eggs upwards into floating plants. The sticky eggs remain in the plants until they hatch. It is very difficult to raise the young due to their extremely small size. The best the aquarist can do is to feed them infusoria and hope they'll survive. Once the fishes reach a size where they can take newly hatched brine shrimp, they'll be well on their way to adulthood.

When they grow to adults, glassfishes develop an indentation in the forehead. As the fish ages, this indentation becomes more pronounced.

Glassfish at first appear to be relatively simple to care for. In reality, however, they are one of the most difficult species to maintain for any reasonable length of time. Live foods are a necessity for good health and even for survival in some individuals. For a time live brine shrimp will do, but after a while they seem to tire of it. All individuals we have kept have ignored fruitflies but occasionally took white worms. In general, the more varied the diet the better the chances for success.

The glassfishes then are probably not a good choice for a community tank. They are timid and are very finicky eaters. They do not do well with larger fishes and seem to get lost in a large tank, unless, of course, you have a large school of them. If the aquarist wants to set up a small tank and can devote a lot of time to it, glassfishes are a good choice.

DATNIOIDES SPECIES

Datnioides species are the largest brackish water fishes commonly kept. The Siamese tiger fish, *Datnioides quadrifasciatus,* is the one usually seen in shops. While it is an impressive fish, the aquarist should take several things into account before adding it to a tank. It is a large fish, sometimes reaching up to 10 inches in length. While it looks small and meek at the three-inch size usually seen in shops it actually turns out to be very active and has a tremendous appetite. It not only keeps smaller fishes away from food, but often makes a meal of them.

If the aquarist has a large enough tank (55 gallons or larger) and is planning on keeping only large fishes that can take care of themselves, then the *Datnioides* are beautiful

1

2 3

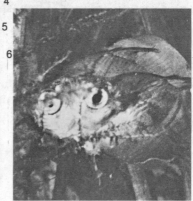

This series of photos shows the courting and spawning of the glassfish *Chanda ranga.* The male is the fish with the light borders on the soft part of the dorsal fin and on the anal fin. He chases the female into thickets of plants (1, 2, 3, 4 and 5). Then, side by side, the fish quiver as many eggs are expelled and fertilized (6 and 7). Photos by R. Zukal.

additions. In general we cannot recommend them for the brackish water community tank.

MONODACTYLUS SPECIES

These are probably the best known of all brackish water aquarium fishes and are about as close to being perfect brackish aquarium residents as one can get. With an angelfish-like body, it has the distinction of having scales on the dorsal and anal fins.

When choosing specimens, the aquarist should place himself in front of the tank for several minutes and watch each fish. If all of them look fine, have the shopkeeper net the number desired. Then stand back and have a good laugh, because *Monodactylus argenteus* is without a doubt the hardest fish in the hobby to get into a net. If some look less than perfect, then pick out the specific ones you want and have the shopkeeper net them. But do not allow your eyes to leave the desired fish once the chase is on, because it will immediately change appearance and you'll never find it again.

In selecting the fish, avoid all-black specimens. When in distress, *Monodactylus argenteus* blacken. This is normal when they are being transported or chased with a net, but a fish that is black when you see it in the dealer's tank and before it has been chased probably has a problem. It could be something as minor as water that is too cool or a sudden movement outside the tank, but as a beginner it is better not to take a chance. During the years of experience behind this book, we have purchased many black specimens, and I can honestly say I've had very good luck with the ones I did buy, but until you know the species intimately, it is better to pass them up.

A healthy *Monodactylus argenteus* has a high shape that resembles an adult tinfoil barb. The dorsal fin, anal fin and part of the tail are canary yellow. There are two black lines running vertically, one through the eye and one through the edge of the gill plate. In healthy adult specimens, the eyes are often sky blue.

A *Monodactylus sebae* has a body that tends to be more greyish than silver. A shiny silver individual, however, does occasionally occur, and this is not a sign of ill health.

One, two or three monos per tank is not a good choice. One alone harasses the other tank occupants; two or three often establish a pecking order in which underlings are sometimes bullied unmercifully. With a group of four or more the monos school peacefully. The greater their numbers, the more peaceful they are and the more dramatic the display. Even in schools, some *Monodactylus sebae* can be aggressive toward much smaller fishes.

All in all, *M. argenteus* is one of the best brackish water fishes. They are beautiful, hearty eaters and can take care of themselves without being aggressive . . . truly the perfect fish. *Monodactylus sebae* is a little less perfect than *M. argenteus*, being a little less hardy and a little harder to feed, but is still an excellent fish for a large tank.

ARCHERFISHES

There are several species of archers, with *Toxotes jaculator* being the most common. While *T. jaculator* gets to be a large fish, it really does not need a large tank, as it is not very active. In nature, most of the archer's time is spent hanging just below the surface of the water waiting for an insect to light on an overhanging twig. Even in the aquarium, where there are no overhanging twigs, its behavior is about the same.

Archers should always be kept one to a tank. Although they are very peaceful toward other fishes, including fishes much smaller than themselves, they do not get along with others of their own species once they reach adulthood.

Archers are not beautiful fishes and are kept mainly as a novelty. Their marksmanship is well known. The tongue and the roof of the mouth are modified into a device for shooting droplets of water at insects. Adults can make accurate shots in excess of four feet. This is especially amazing when one considers the refraction of light as it crosses the air-water interface.

Tanks containing archerfishes should always be securely covered. Archers have been known to jump out of the water after food, and they often shoot water at passing images, even though the image may be the fish's owner rather than an insect.

Archers are native to mangrove swamps nearly all over Asia and Australia. As such, they require fairly warm water (80°) and can do well without heavy aeration.

SCATS

Scats are also very popular brackish water fishes. There are two common varieties, the green scat *(Scatophagus argus)* and the red scat *(Scatophagus argus* var. *rubrifons.)* The green scat is beautiful at all stages. The color pattern of black polka dots on the shiny green background appears when the fish is very young and remains throughout its life. In the red scat, the dots are a brownish color on a red background. As a juvenile, the fish is one of the most beautiful of all. But as it ages, the dots become less distinct splotches and the red often washes out to a reddish brown.

It is almost unheard of to get a scat that won't eat. They are notorius gluttons and often resort to eating even mud. They are heavy plant eaters, so they are best kept in an unplanted tank and given a regular vegetable supplement in the diet.

Found in the areas around Southeast Asia to New Guinea and Australia, scats attain an adult size of up to 12 inches. Large specimens need saltier water than small ones.

While scats are not as showy as monos, they are just as hardy and can tolerate a great deal of stress. They can take care of themselves if need be but are basically peaceful fishes.

(1) Another brackish water sleeper goby is *Dormitator maculatus.* Photo by G. Timmerman. Juvenile scats are seen in several different color patterns from spotted (2) to spotted and striped (3; photo by E. Bates).

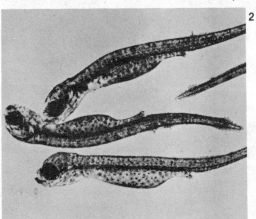

1

2

(1) Pipefishes are
found in brackish
estuaries and bays
in temperate and
tropical areas of the
world. Photo by
R.P.L. Straughan. (2)
Newborn pipefishes.
Photo by A. Van
Den Nieuwenhuizen.

BUMBLEBEE GOBY

These are among the most beautiful of all brackish aquarium fishes, rivaling many of the marine reef species in color. The two most common species, *Brachygobius xanthozonus* and *B. nunus*, are small, peaceful bottom feeders with very large mouths. Adult specimens seldom exceed one-and-one-half inches, yet somehow these miniature fishes have gained a reputation as fish killers. Contrary to claims, they obviously do not kill and swallow monos or scats!

These peaceful little fishes are visible in the aquarium constantly. Much of the bumblee goby's time is spent hopping rather than swimming from place-to-place along the gravel, looking for morsels of food. At other times it is seen stuck to the glass sides of the tank. The ventral fins form a suction disk that enables these fishes to remain in such a position without effort for extended periods of time.

Even though they are bottom feeders, as scavengers bumblebee gobies are far from ideal. Their tastes are simply too picky. But their great looks make them favorites among brackish water hobbyists, and because of their small size, gobies are ideal for small brackish water tanks.

When purchasing a bumblebee goby check the coloration, for it is the best indicator of health. A healthy bumblebee goby has alternating canary yellow and black bands with distinct edges on each band. If the bands appear gray and beige, the fish may be in poor health.

PUFFERS

The family Tetraodontidae contains all the brackish and saltwater puffers. There are a large number of marine species, most of which are considerably larger than the small brackish species. Three species are commonly kept in home aquaria and are usually easy to find in shops. In addition, several other small species are occasionally available. For the brackish water novice, it would be better to stick to the common types until a basic knowledge of the puffers is obtained.

Puffers generally have bodies that are covered by tiny modified scales, and they appear to be scaleless, but of course they are not. The brackish water species have small retractable spines on a portion of the underside of their bodies. The family name comes from the fact that they possess four fused teeth that are modified into a beak-like structure. Puffers are basically carnivorous, although the leopard puffer *(Tetraodon schoutedeni)* does require some vegetable matter for good health.

Although the small brackish water puffers appear to be lethargic, slow moving fishes, close observation shows that they are very active. Due to the unusual structure-function relationship of the fins, the puffers have to work hard to make what little movement they do. Propulsion comes mainly from the pectoral fins with some assistance from the dorsal and anal fins which undulate rapidly and help propel the fish. The caudal fin, which provides forward thrust in most fish, is used exclusively for steering in pufferfishes, exactly as a rudder is used on a sailboat.

Pufferfishes endear themselves to their owners faster than just about any fish in the hobby. In addition to their strange mode of locomotion, they have a habit that most fanciers fall in love with. Puffers have hearty appetites and will eat as long as food is available. A common sight shortly after feeding time is to see a round little fish resting on the bottom of the tank totally helpless. It rolls with the currents and is sometimes tossed around the tank bottom like a ball. This formerly slim fish is unable to move for several hours after a heavy feeding.

In addition to its endearing habits, puffers seem to possess a personality that is unique in the fish world. Their adorable little faces seem to show emotion, and when their faces don't, their antics do. In order to fully understand them, one would have to take the time to make friends with a puffer. It is time well spent.

Many persons are familiar with the puffers' peculiar habit of inflating the body with water or air when alarmed. This causes the spines on the underside to stand erect and makes the fish an undesirable mouthful. When lifted out of the water, they express their discontent by clicking or grunting loudly. It should be kept in mind that while these actions may be interesting to observe, it is cruel to alarm the fish for the purpose of viewing the display. In addition, young specimens can sustain severe or fatal damage by inflating.

Feeding puffers can be a problem, because they have voracious appetites and they love live food. The simplest solution we have found actually rids us of another problem. The snails that wreak havoc in our tanks are relished by puffers. They are literally an unlimited source of live food. Adult puffers can crush the shells with their beak-like teeth, but juvenile specimens need help from the aquarist.

Puffers have a reputation for being fin nippers. While they are occasionally aggressive toward each other, they do not bother other fishes. Even aggression among their own kind is not dangerous. It is more like wrestling than fighting.

The green puffer *(Tetraodon fluviatilis)* is found from India to Malaya and the Philippines. Its entire life is spent in brackish and occasionally fresh water.

The leopard puffer *(Tetraodon schoutedeni)* is found in the Congo in large quantities and less frequently in other places. It is usually found only in freshwater.

My favorite of all brackish water fishes is the figure eight puffer *(Tetraodon palembangensis)*. This species is one of the most beautiful of all fishes. The back is light metallic green with a dark green figure eight superimposed. The bottom half of the body is pure white. The sides are sometimes dotted with small dark green circles with light green in the center.

1
2
3

4

5   6

(1) A warm-water sole, *Achirus* species. (2) *Anableps anableps* peering out of the water. Photo by W. Twomey. (3) A lateral view of *Anableps*. Photo by Dr. Herbert R. Axelrod at the Berlin Aquarium. (4) *Tetraodon palembangensis,* common in the aquarium trade. (5) Another common hobby puffer is *Tetraodon schoutedeni.* Photo by A. Noznov. (6) Puffers are gluttonous eaters.

The only disease that has proven to be a problem for us in keeping puffers has been hemorrhaging of the skin. Once this hemorrhaging has begun, the fish invariably dies.

In all, puffers are great fishes for brackish water aquaria. They are seldom more than two inches long and are very attractive. Their good behavior makes them safe with almost any other fishes, and their great personality makes them an excellent pet. They can handle themselves well with large fishes like monos and scats, yet are the ideal size for small aquaria. The puffers are a perfect addition to any brackish water tank.

LIVEBEARERS

The first exposure most aquarists have to brackish water fishes usually occurs when they bring home their first molly. In general, they are not only unaware that the fish needs brackish water, but are unaware of what brackish water is. Many guppy hobbyists add salt to their water to obtain the healthiest fish possible and occasionally other hobbyists will salt the water of other livebearers, but the true brackish water livebearers are the halfbeaks and the mollies.

There are several species of halfbeaks, with *Dermogenys pusillus* being the most common. Halfbeaks are found in the Malay Peninsula and are used in gambling in Southeast Asia, where they are bred for their fighting ability similar to the way bettas are exploited for gambling. The females reach a length of about three inches, but the males remain a bit smaller.

In the aquarium halfbeaks spend a good portion of their time hanging motionless beneath the surface of the water. Although they are bred to fight each other in some areas, they are very peaceful toward other species, and even among themselves damage is rarely done. Their combat is more sparring than contact fighting.

Halfbeaks are difficult to breed. They deliver living young every 28 to 30 days and are very cannibalistic. A

1

3

2

4

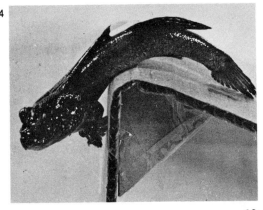

(1, 2, 3 and 4) A mudskipper, *Periophthalmus* species, shows its natural acrobatics on a cardboard ramp. Mudskippers come out of their brackish water habitats to hunt for food. Photos by L. Hess.

1 2

3

4

(1) A mudskipper collects some water from which it extracts oxygen while on land. (2) *Periophthalmus barbatus* rests on a leaf. Photo by H. Hansen, Aquarium Berlin. (3) The mudskipper rests on stones. (4) Using its pelvic suction discs, mudskippers can climb up an aquarium wall. (5) Mudskippers look for food out of water. Photos 1, 3, 4 and 5 by Jorgen Hansen.

5

(1) Giant sailfin mollies such as this *Poecilia velifera* are found in fresh and brackish waters in lagoons, estuaries and streams mainly in the coastal areas of Yucatan in southeastern Mexico. Males reach six inches in length and females reach eight inches. These are the largest of all the mollies. Photo by R. Zukal. (2) There are two common species of *Monodactylus;* they are *M. sebae* and *M. argenteus.* This is a young *M. argenteus.* Photo by M. Chvojka.

breeding trap is nearly impossible to use since the young are often born over a period of several days. The litters are small with ten to 40 being normal, depending upon the quality and quantity of food the mother receives.

Males of *D. pusillus* possess a red spot on the dorsal and anal fins. A smaller species, *Dermogenys sumatranus* from Singapore, Sumatra and Borneo, is sometimes available. It is more brownish and lacks black or red stripes on the lower jaw. Brightly colored *Nomorhamphus* species from the Celebes are becoming available also.

Mollies are one of the four major groups of livebearers that have been selectively bred into countless varities. In my opinion the breeding of fancy livebearers is the most advanced form of aquarium keeping. These fishes offer the greatest challenge of any in the hobby. Whereas in other fishes the challenge is to reproduce the size and coloring of the parents, in fancy livebearers the challenge is to constantly introduce new color and finnage forms. The work is harder, but the rewards are greater.

The mollies are the least varied of the fancy livebearers but there are still as many varieties available as an aquarist could ever need. Wild mollies are usually green but a black shows up occasionally. The tank bred varieties are seen in gold, albino, red, chocolate, marbled, liberty and many others. Two types of finnage occur naturally in mollies, the short fins of *Poecelia (Mollienisia) sphenops* and the sailfin variety. The fancy finnage in mollies however, is somewhat limited. The first to be developed was the lyretail. Mollies have the only true rounded lyretail in the hobby. Swordtails, guppies and platies have simple tail extensions that are called lyretails, but they lack the true lyre shape. Most lyretails possess a differently shaped dorsal fin than that of the wild type. The fin seems to be shorter from front to back at the base. Another recent introduction has been mollies with tassles. These are elongations of the ventral fins to over an inch in length.

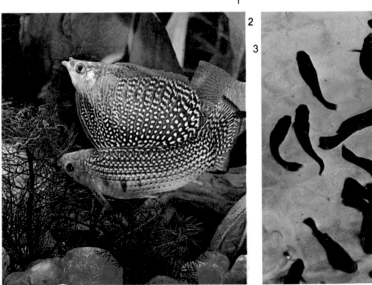

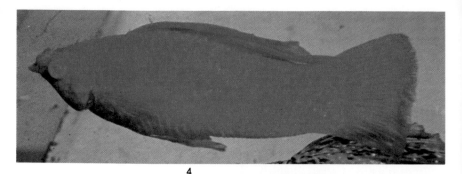

4

5

Mollies have long been an aquarium favorite. Sailfin mollies are available in a number of color strains such as black (1), red (4), albino (6) and the wild strain (2). Black mollies (3, 5) were the first all-black fishes to come into the tropical fish hobby. Photo 1 by H.J. Richter. Photo 4 by Y.W. Ong. Photo 5 by Dr. Herbert R. Axelrod.

6

Recently a new characteristic, the veiltail, was introduced. As of this writing the veiltail trait is nearly impossible to find, as it has not yet been firmly established. Those maintaining the strains seem to be keeping them to themselves and as a result the establishment of the veiltail may be slow in coming. Veiltail mollies are very expensive, usually being about $40.00 a pair when available.

Mollies need a large amount of vegetable matter for maintaining good health. For breeding purposes they should be kept in bare tanks with no other species. Pregnant females should always be moved from tank to tank in a bottle (if they have to be moved) rather than netted to avoid stressing them and causing premature birth. Females cannot tolerate breeding traps and should be kept in well aerated tanks of at least three gallons capacity. The tank should be filled to the top with floating plants such as *Elodea*. When the female has finished delivering, she should be removed but not placed with males for two or three days. With the females gone, the plants can then be removed to give the young swimming room.

In raising the young, culling is necessary. It is difficult for the beginner to cull effectively until the fish are nearly full-grown. Here are some tips to help. Always discard fishes with deformed spines or those that can't get off the bottom. Deformed spines can be hereditary and do not improve. If allowed to breed, the trait can be passed on to the young. A fish not being able to get off the bottom suggests swim bladder damage. Again, it will not improve. Early developing males should be discarded, because it has been shown that young males showing early signs of sexual maturity are likely to be dwarfed. Only the late developing males are going to reach full size. Mollies are born with their adult color and that color will not change later. If breeding for a special color, all not possessing it at birth should be discarded. Culling for finnage is virtually impossible until adulthood. As a result, mollies tie up a great

1

2

Lyretail black
mollies (2) were
probably derived
from *Poecilia
sphenops* (1).
Photo 1 by Dr.
Herbert R. Axelrod.

3

4

(1, 2) The bright spotted pattern of the scat, *Scatophagus argus,* has made it a favorite among brackish water aquarium hobbyists. Photo 2 by H.J. Richter. (3) *Monodactylus argenteus* lacks the mid-body vertical bar seen in *M. sebae* (4). Photo 3 by Aaron Norman. Photo 4 by H. Azuma.

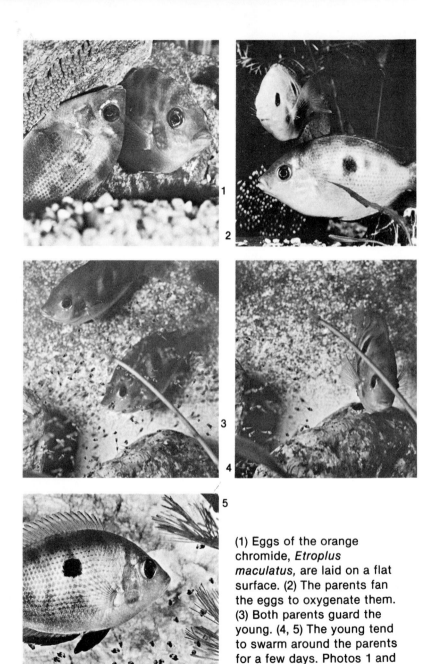

(1) Eggs of the orange chromide, *Etroplus maculatus,* are laid on a flat surface. (2) The parents fan the eggs to oxygenate them. (3) Both parents guard the young. (4, 5) The young tend to swarm around the parents for a few days. Photos 1 and 5 by K. Nilsson. Photo 2 by H.J. Richter. Photos 3 and 4 by G. Marcuse.

deal of tank space for the serious hobbyist. Since no more than six adults should be kept in a thirty-gallon tank, and no adult should be kept in anything smaller than a thirty, raising mollies is a major project. The real beauty of a good exotic mollie, however, makes it all worthwhile.

MISCELLANEOUS FISHES

There are some other commonly kept brackish water fishes that were not mentioned under any of the previous headings. A fairly common one is the orange chromide *(Etroplus maculatus)*, an Asian dwarf cichlid. There are some African brackish water cichlids also, but the Asian orange chromide is the only one commonly kept, as it is very peaceful and hardy. In nature it lives in coastal portions of rivers, so it can tolerate severe changes in salinity as well as temperature. Due to its small size (under three inches), the orange chromide is the perfect fish for the small brackish aquarium, but it is well able to handle itself in the large aquarium as well.

A slightly less common group of brackish water fishes are the rainbowfishes. The Queensland rainbow *(Melanotaenia maccullochi)* is a very small, three-inch fish with reddish brown stripes over an olive base. The somewhat larger (six inches) Australian rainbow *(M. nigans)* is a silver color that reflects rainbow tints from its foil-like scales. When full-grown and properly illuminated, the Australian rainbow is truly a beautiful fish. It is very active, especially when kept in a school of six or more. Both of these rainbowfishes are peaceful and hardy, and both are very prolific—they are good spawners for beginners.

A species of flatfish commonly sold as a flounder is more than likely the sole *Trinectes maculatus*. It is usually sold at a size of one inch but can reach a length of five or six inches under ideal conditions. Its good points are numerous; it is hardy, a good scavenger, peaceful and has some interesting

(1) A brackish water goby that is fairly peaceful is *Gobioides broussonneti.* Photo by Ted Angel. The diamond killifish (2), *Adinia xenica,* and the American flagfish (4), *Jordanella floridae,* are brackish water killifishes. *Ameca splendens* (3) is a brackish water and freshwater livebearing goodeid. Photo 2 by A. Norman. Photo 3 by Ruth Brewer. Photo 4 by H.J. Richter.

3

4

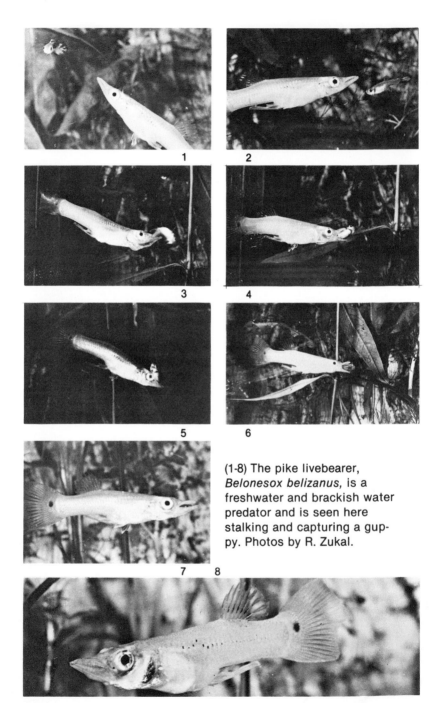

(1-8) The pike livebearer, *Belonesox belizanus*, is a freshwater and brackish water predator and is seen here stalking and capturing a guppy. Photos by R. Zukal.

habits. Although this species seems to be an ideal aquarium fish, unfortunately it is rarely seen in pet shops. If the tank has natural gravel in it, the color pattern of the fish will coincide exactly with that of the substrate making it difficult to see. If the gravel is variously colored, the fish tries to match each color, coming closest to black. Needless to say, the problems of trying to match a red or blue background color places the fish under undue stress and should be avoided.

At times, the flatfish may stick themselves to the aquarium glass giving an observer a closeup look at the pale side. At other times they completely bury themselves in the gravel. We have found them to be very easy to keep, doing well in both large and small tanks. To date, though, we have not been successful in putting any appreciable size on a specimen. We have kept some for over a year with no noticeable growth even though the tank was heavily fed and much food fell to the bottom.

There are many killies that would go well in the smaller brackish water aquarium such as the Florida flagfish *Jordanella floridae,* the diamond killie, *Adinia xenica,* and the sheepshead, *Cyrpinodon variegatus.*

Occasionally a brackish water fish is sold exclusively as a marine fish. An example is the damsel *Neopomacentrus taeniurus.* Many of the plainer marine gobies, especially from northern waters, are actually brackish water fishes. They are too numerous to mention here and are not commonly seen anyway. The marine shop-owner may not have them properly identified, so it is up to the aquarist to make the identification and determination of suitability prior to purchase.

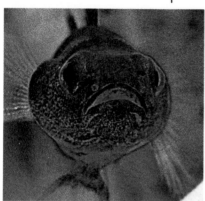

(1) The bumblebee goby male flashes his colors to the dull colored female. (2) The male chooses a shell or cave as his territory. (3) Eggs are laid and fertilized in the chosen shell. (4) The male guards the eggs stuck to the inside of the shell cave. (5) The male courts the female at the entrance of his shell cave. Photos by H.J. Richter.

Poecilia vivipara is one of the many less colorful livebearers found in brackish swamps and streams. Photo by G. Timmerman. In the photo below the female pike livebearer shows a distinct horizontal stripe. Photo by M. Chvojka.

A Few Closing Comments

In closing this book, I would like to repeat some of the finer points of the fishes already covered and give a few examples of good community aquariums.

Datnioides do not get along with any of the other common fishes and are best left to themselves. Monos should always be kept in schools. Scats and mollies should not be kept in a planted tank. Glassfish should not be kept with larger fishes.

Keeping these thoughts in mind, the following possibilities are practical:

3

4

(1) The Siamese tiger fish, *Datnioides microlepis,* is a large ferocious predator. Photo by P. Tsang. (2) Sleeper gobies often assume odd postures. (3) *Etroplus suratensis* is known as the green chromide. Photo by Dr. Herbert R. Axelrod. (4) A male orange chromide shows his breeding colors. Photo by H.J. Richter.

10-GALLON TANK

1 Glassfish
4 Bumblebee gobies
2 Halfbeaks
1 Flounder
1 Puffer
2 or 3 Killies
1 Orange chromide

20-GALLON TANK

2 Mollies
2 Queensland rainbows
2 Orange chromides
4 Bumblebee gobies
1 or 2 Puffers

30-GALLON TANK

4 *Monodactylus argenteus*
1 Archer
1 Scat
4 Bumblebee gobies
2 Puffers
2 Australian Rainbows
1 Flounder

55-GALLON TANK

6 Monos (either species)
1 Archer
4 Scats
8 Bumblebee gobies
2 Flounders
4 Australian rainbows
4 Puffers

100-GALLON TANK

20 Monos (any combination)
1 Archer
6 Scats
12 Bumblebee gobies
6 Puffers
8 Australian rainbows
6 Orange chromides

The above communities are only suggestions showing possibilities and load limits. Virtually unlimited combinations can be worked out. If you happen to prefer scats to monos then switch their numbers in the 100-gallon tank, If an attempt is made to match fishes' needs as listed in the previous chapters, almost any combination will be successful.

We have been tremendously pleased with the growth of the brackish hobby since our first article on our research gained national attention in 1973. It is our hope that this interest will grow to the magnitude it deserves. We should no longer break aquarium keeping into just freshwater or marine disciplines, but should also add the third option—brackish water.